IT'S ALL HERE!

Any *real* wrestling fan knows what makes wrestling the exciting, interesting, thrilling sport it is. It's not just the incredible matches, the awesome champions, and the baddest bad guys around. It's the weird moments you remember—the times when everything doesn't go quite the way it should and the outcome is totally unpredictable!

This book gives you a collection of stories about just those events. The strange, the amazing, the odd, and the unbelievable—they're all here for you in . . .

STRANGE AND AMAZING
WRESTLING STORIES

Books by Bill Gutman

STRANGE AND AMAZING WRESTLING STORIES
Sports Illustrated/STRANGE AND AMAZING FOOTBALL
  STORIES
Sports Illustrated/GREAT MOMENTS IN PRO FOOTBALL
REFRIGERATOR PERRY

Available from ARCHWAY paperbacks

STRANGE & AMAZING WRESTLING STORIES

Bill Gutman

AN ARCHWAY PAPERBACK
Published by POCKET BOOKS • NEW YORK

Interior photographs by George Napolitano

AN ARCHWAY PAPERBACK *Original*

 An Archway Paperback published by
POCKET BOOKS, a division of Simon & Schuster, Inc.
1230 Avenue of the Americas, New York, N.Y. 10020

ISBN: 0-671-61134-8

First Archway Paperback printing May, 1986

10 9 8 7 6 5 4

AN ARCHWAY PAPERBACK and colophon are
registered trademarks of Simon & Schuster, Inc.

Printed in the U.S.A.

IL 4+

CONTENTS

CONTENTS

STRANGE & AMAZING
AMAZING

WRESTLING
STORIES

Sergeant Slaughter makes a brash prediction before entering ring for tag team Battle Royal.

SERGEANT SLAUGHTER
STANDS ALONE

Sergeant Slaughter has fought many an epic battle during his years as a professional wrestler. Once a chronic rulebreaker and villain, the venerable Sarge changed his tune when the big influx of anti-American wrestlers began. Taking a cue from his years as a tough U.S. Marine Corps drill instructor, the Sarge decided it was time for someone to stand up for the Stars and Stripes.

Slowly but surely, Sergeant Slaughter shed his bad-guy image and won legions of new and loyal fans, who loved to see the near-300-pounder do battle with the enemies of the United States. But with all his ring wars throughout the country, the Sarge never stood taller than he did in 1985 when he was part of the Star Wars '85 extravaganza at New Jersey's Meadowlands Arena.

The Sarge was entered in an amazing match, aptly named the Battle Royal. There would be twelve tag teams in the ring at one time. And for those without a calculator, that means twenty-four wrestlers all causing mayhem at once. A team was eliminated anytime one of its members was thrown from the ring. And it would continue until just one team remained. Among those participating were such top-rated combos as the Road Warriors, Jerry Lawler and Baron Von Raschke, the Youngbloods, Ivan and Nikita Koloff, Jimmy Valiant and Bob Backland, Kamala and Billy Robinson, and Larry Zbyszko and Jimmy Garvin.

Why were so many outstanding tag teams joining in a Battle Royal that could prove brutal and dangerous? Simple. The prize for the winning team was a whopping $100,000! All the wrestlers could taste the money, including Sergeant Slaughter, who was teaming with 400-pound Jerry "Crusher" Blackwell.

As the teams for the Battle Royal were introduced, the Road Warriors and the Slaughter-Blackwell team came in last. But something was wrong. Jerry Blackwell was dressed in street clothes! The Sarge entered the ring and grabbed the microphone. He informed the huge crowd that Blackwell was injured and unable to wrestle. But not to worry. Sergeant Slaughter wasn't about to disappoint his fans. He would still compete, going it alone against eleven of the best tag-team combos in the country!

The fans roared. It was a courageous act. But how could one man, no matter how tough, withstand the onslaught of the top twelve tag teams in the country? After all, the Battle Royal depended on teamwork, two wrestlers working together to get rid of opponents

2

while protecting each other at the same time. But the proud and tough Sergeant Slaughter was about to try.

At the bell, all mayhem broke loose in the ring. Some tag teams went after heated rivals, like the Koloffs attacking the Road Warriors, while others just tried to survive and stay in the match. When Mr. Saito and the Masked Superstar went after Greg Gagne and Jim Brunzell, the Sarge went to their aid, jumping the Masked Superstar, a wrestler he does not like.

There were teams being eliminated every few minutes, but the Sarge held on, despite taking a bad beating from several teams trying to gang up on him. Finally there were four teams left: Kamala and Robinson, Lawler and the Baron, the Road Warriors . . . and Sergeant Slaughter. Now the Road Warriors came after the Sarge. They trapped him in the corner, intent on tossing his considerable bulk out of the ring. But just as it seemed he was going over the top rope, Sergeant Slaughter summoned some superhuman strength and not only held onto the rope, but somehow maneuvered both Road Warriors over his back and out of the ring.

While that was happening, Kamala and Robinson had eliminated Lawler and the Baron. As the Sarge turned to face the enemy again, the crowd began chanting—U-S-A, U-S-A, U-S-A—trying to urge the ex-marine on. Kamala, a giant Ugandan weighing in at more than 350 pounds who teamed with British Commonwealth champ Robinson, looked to end it as he turned his evil eyes on the Sarge.

Prospects seemed bleak when Kamala chopped the

The feared Road Warriors, with their manager, Paul Ellering, were one of the favored teams entering the Battle Royal.

American to his knees and Robinson began to kick at him. When the two double-flipped the Sarge, the match appeared all but over. Sergeant Slaughter had put up a valiant battle, but the odds were just too high.

Still the crowd hadn't quit. The chants of *U-S-A* continued to grow louder. To Sergeant Slaughter, it must have sounded like the bugles trumpeting a charge. It was as if the Sarge suddenly had the fate of the whole country before him. He had to overcome this foreign assault.

Where the strength came from, no one will ever know. But suddenly there was Sergeant Slaughter, smashing Robinson to the canvas. He then took off after Kamala and battered the giant across the ring.

Finally he was ready to unleash the Slaughter cannon. In rapid succession, both Kamala and Robinson went flying from the ring. When the match had begun, twenty-three wrestlers entered the ring together, but now Sergeant Slaughter stood alone, winner of the Battle Royal and of $100,000.

Even though Kamala and Robinson soon returned to the ring and whipped an unsuspecting Slaughter into the turnbuckle, cutting open his head, nothing could dim the achievement of the patriotic American. Once order had been restored, Sergeant Slaughter stood in the center of the ring, his head bleeding, and led the crowd in reciting the Pledge of Allegiance to the Flag.

"You have just witnessed one of the greatest performances in wrestling history," said the Sarge's injured partner, Jerry Blackwell.

As for Slaughter, he could only say this: "When I saw all those people waving their flags, and heard them chant *U-S-A, U-S-A*, tears came to my eyes. They were tears of pride, in America and the American people."

For Sergeant Slaughter, it was an amazing moment he would never forget.

THE HULK'S GREATEST SLAM

Perhaps the most popular and charismatic wrestler of the 1980s is Hulk Hogan. The 6'8" 300-pounder is a product of muscle beach in California, where he hones his rock-hard body through dedicated weight training.

When the Hulk first began grappling in the squared circle, he was more or less a rulebreaker, and not always willing to court the fancy of the fans. But by the time he donned a simple but effective MADE IN AMERICA T-shirt, the Hulk began his rise to the top. Before long, he was not only the new World Wrestling Federation champion, defeating the villainous Iron Sheik for the title, but was also the new darling of the fans. Hulkamania had been born.

Once he was champ, everyone naturally wanted a shot at the Hulk. Because of his huge size and strength, many of his opponents were dwarfed and intimidated by the amazing Hulkster. But as they say, no matter how big, how strong, how fast, there is always someone bigger, stronger, faster. One of those clamoring to meet the Hulk was the hated Big John Studd, all 6'10" and 360 pounds of him.

Studd was the self-proclaimed "biggest, meanest, and baddest" dude in all of wrestling, and he wanted to prove it against the Hulkster, with the WWF championship at stake. Finally the match was set for September 1984, and the two met before a sellout crowd at Madison Square Garden in New York City.

The match was even at the outset, but turned when Studd managed to put a sleeper hold on the champ. Using his immense strength, the Hulk somehow broke the hold, something very few wrestlers were able to do against Big John. But the sleeper had weakened the Hulk and Studd wasn't one to waste an advantage.

Before the Hulkster could recover, Studd picked him up like a ragdoll and tossed him out of the ring. Dazed and bleeding, the Hulk tried to regain his senses as his legions of fans looked on in disbelief. But he couldn't get back into the ring and the referee counted him out. Hulk Hogan had been defeated.

There was one catch. According to the rules of professional wrestling, the championship can only change hands on a pin. Though the Hulk lost the match, he did not lose his title. Within minutes, Big John Studd was demanding a rematch. If he could beat the Hulk one way, reasoned Big John, he could pin him the next time.

Embarrassed by his defeat and not one to refuse a challenge, the Hulk agreed to meet Studd for a second time. Big John even sweetened the rematch pot. He told the Hulkster he would give him $15,000 if the champ could bodyslam him. No one, he said, had ever bodyslammed Big John Studd.

When the rematch took place several weeks later, there was a huge crowd on hand and they began chanting for the Hulk as soon as the match began. Perhaps the Hulk was too concerned with the bodyslam challenge, for several times early in the match he tried to position Studd for a slam, but Big John foiled them all. In fact, one of the slam attempts really backfired and Studd began beating the Hulk with his fists. Once again the Hulk was stunned. The fans were suddenly silent. Was history going to repeat? Would Big John Studd again defeat the mighty Hulk? And this time, would he win the title by a pin?

Then the Hulkster rallied. After Studd missed a karate chop to the neck, the Hulk came back, stunning Big John with several powerful arm chops and then a kick to the head. Now the crowd was back in the match, shouting for the Hulk to bodyslam his opponent. The champ tried to oblige, but Studd was ready. He slammed his fists into Hogan's head and sent the Hulk to the canvas in a daze.

The match continued in seesaw fashion, each of the giants taking turns pummeling the other. But in lunging at Studd for another slam attempt, the Hulk slipped through the ropes and hit his head on the announcer's table. Blood spurted from the wound, obscuring the Hulk's vision. Studd was quick to take advantage and slammed the champ's head against the metal corner of the ring. Then he grabbed the Hulk and tossed him back into the ring. The champion was almost helpless, flat on his stomach as Studd leaped from the ropes onto the Hulk's back. It looked all but over.

Twice Studd tried to pin the Hulk, but both times the mighty Hulk kicked out of it, encouraged by the crowd. Studd, however, continued to hand out punishment. He slammed Hogan to the canvas, then drop-kicked the champ right out of the ring. It began to look like a replay of their first match.

As the Hulk tried to get back into the ring, Studd kicked at him again, only this time the champ caught his foot and pulled Big John out of the ring with him. Studd immediately resumed his pounding, but the roar of the crowd and the mystique known as Hulkamania suddenly took hold. Without warning, Hulk Hogan dropped his hands and shouted at Studd.

"Go on, hit me with your best shot!"

Big John took a swing, but the champ blocked it and slammed Studd hard in the forehead. The big man reeled from the blow and the Hulk sprang forward like a cat. Almost effortlessly, he hoisted the 360-pound challenger over his head and slammed him hard to the concrete floor outside the ring.

Studd didn't move. He was finished. With the roar of the crowd still ringing in his ear, Hulk Hogan waved his championship belt in the air. He had picked up the gauntlet and successfully defended his title, accomplishing in the process something that no one had ever done before. He had bodyslammed Big John Studd, to add still another chapter to the amazing legend of Hulkamania.

WHO IS THAT MASKED MAN?

Who is that masked man? That was a question asked over and over again during the long run of the popular masked hero, the Lone Ranger, on both radio and television. But it's also been asked many times over the years about certain professional wrestlers who choose to hide their faces from the general public.

Many grapplers have worn masks in the ring. Some just want to scare their opponents by taking on a sinister masked look. Others reveal their identities, but not their faces, to ensure privacy in their lives outside the squared circle. But a few defy convention. They keep their true identities a mystery, their backgrounds secret. They taunt their opponents into trying to unmask them, and will fight with unabashed fury to keep their faces covered.

In the late 1950s, an American wrestler named Doctor Death traveled to England to ply his trade. He continued grappling in the British Isles for years, defying anyone to unmask him or to discover his identity. It was a mystery that drove opponents and fans crazy. Though just 5'10" and 210 pounds, Doctor Death was a man who was not only difficult to defeat, but impossible to unmask.

His British promoter had this to say about the American expatriate. "He is one of the best in the world. He's fought the best and never been beaten. And there isn't a wrestler around who wouldn't love to unmask the bloke. It'll be worth plenty of money to the man who does it."

Between 1957 and 1962, it was estimated that Doctor Death fought and defeated some 1,000 opponents in Continental Europe and Great Britain. But early in 1962, another masked man appeared on the British scene. He called himself the White Angel and pretty soon began to turn his attention to Doctor Death, challenging the American to a match in which the loser would have to remove his mask. Not one to duck a challenge, the Doctor accepted, and the two masked men squared off on April 14, 1962, at the Granada Tooting Arena outside of London.

They battled it out for some 80 minutes, each knowing fully what was at stake if he lost. Finally, though, it was Doctor Death who emerged the winner, and very decisively. The dejected White Angel kept his part of the bargain. He was unmasked in center ring, his identity revealed as Judo Al Hayes, one of the leading judo experts in all of England. And Doctor Death had beaten him in the ring.

So the mystery of Doctor Death continued. He lived a royal life outside, most of it still shrouded in secrecy. Married to a British showgirl, he was reputed to have a valuable art collection and to enjoy the finer things in life. Rumor had it that he was a college-educated intellectual with a darker side that led him to wrestling. But whenever he was asked about his American background or for hints about his identity, the answer was always the same: "It's nobody's business but mine!"

THE FABULOUS MOOLAH

One of the most amazing feats in all of professional wrestling was the reign of the Fabulous Moolah. From 1956 to 1984, Moolah was the undisputed champion of women wrestlers, unbeaten in title matches during that time. Man or woman, no athlete in any individual sport has dominated in quite the same way. The Fabulous Moolah was a one-woman dynasty.

Perhaps the best way to describe Moolah is tough and determined. She's a wrestler who'll do anything to win, no matter what the fans think, and for that reason there were always a lot of people rooting against her. But like her or not, you've got to marvel at the way she stayed at the top of her profession, turning back all challengers for nearly three decades.

Ironically, it was when she finally met defeat that the Fabulous Moolah gained more notoriety than she had in all the years she reigned supreme. In July of 1984, Moolah was scheduled to defend her title again. This

14

New women's champ Wendi Richter and rock star Cyndi Lauper dance around the ring after Richter ended the 28-year championship reign of the Fabulous Moolah in 1984.

time, her opponent was a youngster nicknamed "The Dallas Cowgirl," whose real name was Wendi Richter. It figured to be just another night at the office for Moolah.

But there was a distraction that night. Richter was accompanied by a friend, rock star Cyndi Lauper, who had become one of the top wrestling fans in the country. Richter and Lauper danced into the ring to Lauper's big hit "Girls Just Wanna Have Fun." Moolah glared at them, taking an immediate dislike to Lauper.

Whether she was distracted or not is hard to say. But Moolah finally met her match. Richter pinned the Fabulous One to end her twenty-eight-year record as champion. Moolah fumed. She wanted revenge on both Richter and Lauper.

But thirty years on the circuit is a long time. Though she planned to continue wrestling, Moolah also began managing a newcomer named Lelani Kai. She was totally delighted when Kai defeated Richter to win the title. But when a return match was arranged, the feud between Lauper and Moolah really exploded.

Even before the opening bell, Moolah and Cyndi Lauper were head to head, shouting insults at one another. Once the match started, both Moolah and Lauper began working their way toward each other outside the ring. More fans were watching them than the actual Richter-Kai match in the ring.

Soon the two were pushing and shoving once again, but when Lelani drop-kicked Richter into her corner, Moolah forgot about Cyndi and held onto Richter's legs as Kai punished her with forearm smashes. Suddenly the crowd let out a huge roar, as Lauper smashed Moolah over the head, causing her to release her hold on Richter. Then they wrestled each other to the floor before guards could pull them apart.

Richter eventually won the match, regaining her world title, but even though the Fabulous Moolah was only a manager, she was still the center of attention. Her feud with Lauper will undoubtedly continue and she will keep trying to regain her title.

But no matter which way it turns out, the career and long reign of the Fabulous Moolah has got to be one of the most amazing one-person dynasties in all of sport.

AND IN THIS CORNER, BILLY WHO?

There's an old saying that things aren't always what they seem. Jesse Barr learned exactly what it meant . . . and he learned it the hard way. Barr was Florida State heavyweight champion at one time, and there were a whole group of tough grapplers who wanted his crown. So when Jesse learned he'd be defending his title against an unknown wrestler named Billy Haynes, he figured he deserved an easy match somewhere. Haynes, he reasoned, was an inexperienced newcomer, a sacrificial lamb that Barr could use to sharpen his skills for future tough matches.

But things aren't always what they seem. On the night of the match Barr entered the ring and waited for Billy Haynes. Maybe the youngster wouldn't even show up? Maybe the thought of going up against the champ was too much for him? Barr waited smugly. He wasn't looking when the other wrestler entered the

18

ring, but when he turned around he had to look twice. Then he got mad.

"What are you doing here?" he shouted at the bearded, muscular wrestler facing him. "Get out of the ring. You had your chance already. Tonight it's Billy Haynes's chance."

The other wrestler just grinned.

"I *am* Haynes," he said, laughing.

"What is this, some kind of joke?" Jesse Barr roared back. For the man he was looking at, he knew. It was Billy Jack, a former Florida State champion and one of the strongest, toughest wrestlers around. Jesse Barr wondered all over again. What was Billy Jack standing in the ring for? He was supposed to meet Billy Haynes. Barr was still confused when the referee demanded he get ready to wrestle. At last someone explained it to him. Billy Jack *was* Billy Haynes. Haynes was his real name, and after years of wrestling under the name Billy Jack, Haynes decided to use his real name as a tribute to his sick father. Jesse Barr was the first to know. Or was he the last to know?

Still confused by the sudden turn of events, Barr began the match. But it was the tough Billy Jack . . . er, Billy Haynes, who was doing most of the battering. Barr tried to rally, but the muscular Haynes continued to dominate the match. Finally Barr had had it. Perhaps he felt he had been double-crossed, or because of the Billy Jack–Billy Haynes switch, he couldn't get his mind on the match. Whatever the reason, Jesse Barr decided to walk out. Technically he had lost, but since it wasn't on a pin, he didn't have to give up his Florida State title.

Later Haynes said the name switch wasn't a secret. In fact, he had announced it at a press conference and had written letters to out-of-town media people explaining it. Apparently, however, Barr had never been told.

"No one said a thing to me about him changing his name," Barr said. "Not the promoter, not the National Wrestling Alliance, not the press. Why didn't someone tell me?"

The whole episode wasn't an easy thing for Barr to accept. He felt he had been dealt a low blow, and some say the thought still lingered a few weeks later, when he lost his title to Brian Blair. Whether he will regain the crown or not is uncertain, but one thing is for sure. In the future, Jesse Barr will probably make it his business to know exactly whom he is wrestling. Because he knows now that things aren't always what they seem.

THE 60-SECOND CHAMP

It's one thing to win a championship, and it's another thing to lose it. But when you win it and lose it in the space of just 60 seconds, one minute, well, that's something else again. One of the strangest title matches ever occurred on February 16, 1984, when Sergeant Slaughter challenged Ric Flair for the NWA (National Wrestling Alliance) title at the Civic Center in Baltimore, Maryland.

The match came a year before the Sarge's heroic Battle Royal victory in New Jersey, but the ex-marine was already a popular grappler. The golden-maned Flair had been a busy champion since 1981, defending his title wherever he went. On several occasions when he lost the NWA crown, he came back to regain it.

Before the big match, Sergeant Slaughter told the press how much winning the title meant to him.

"I've fought them all," he said, "everyone from the Sheik to the Superfly, but this is the biggest bout of my entire career. It's been a lifelong dream to be a champion and I plan to leave the ring tonight with the NWA belt in my possession."

As the two gladiators entered the ring, it was obvious that on this particular night the Sarge was the crowd favorite. Referee Tommy Young gave the instructions and the two began to wrestle. Slaughter got the better of it early, but soon Flair began to show why he was the champion, at one point hurling the bigger Sarge clear out of the ring.

While the Sarge lay dazed, Flair strutted around the ring, showing his disdain for his opponent. But once the Sarge got back in, he took charge again, flinging the champ back and forth across the ring and coming close to pinning him several times. Each time Flair escaped, the Sarge became angrier. Finally he flung the exhausted Flair clear across the ring. The champion smashed into referee Young, who crumpled to the mat, semiconscious, while Flair sailed over the top rope. The fans roared. Slaughter was destroying everything in his path.

Still furious, the Sarge leaped out and went after Flair again. They both made it back into the ring as a second referee rushed in to take over for the fallen Tommy Young. Flair was still groggy, and a tremendous elbow smash by the Sarge put the champ in never-never land. Slaughter pounced on him as the ref counted Flair out.

The Sarge jumped for joy. He had done it, defeated Flair for the NWA title. He grabbed the championship

Sergeant Slaughter slams NWA champ Ric Flair to the canvas during their title bout in 1984. The Sarge later pinned Flair and thought he had won the title, only to learn a minute later that he had lost by a controversial disqualification.

belt and waved it to the crowd as he danced around the ring. The fans picked up on the electricity of the moment and went crazy with him. The celebration continued for a full minute, until referee Tommy Young got to his feet and began waving his arms, as if he had something to say.

Then he began talking to the officials at ringside. Suddenly everyone in the arena was quiet. Young was disqualifying Sergeant Slaughter for tossing Ric Flair over the top rope. Flair would retain his championship.

No one could believe it, least of all the Sarge, who had been champ for all of 60 seconds. Now it was being taken from him on a technicality. NWA rules state that tossing your opponent over the top rope means an automatic disqualification. Flair grabbed the belt back from the Sarge, as if to say, hey, you didn't really win this, but the Sarge and his fans knew better.

"I was robbed," the ex-marine said. "I had the man's shoulders pinned. He was beaten. How could they do this to me? The referee who disqualified me was out cold when the whole thing happened. I'm gonna win that belt if it's the last thing I do."

Ric Flair wouldn't forget the match with Sergeant Slaughter for a long time. But at least he came out of it with his title still intact. For the Sarge, it was a moral victory at best, but for 60 seconds he was on top of the world, the champion. Then it all came tumbling down in one of the strangest outcomes of a title match in wrestling history.

HELLO, MR. T

He first made his mark in the movies, appearing as the rough, tough Clubber Lang, who beat up on Sylvester Stallone in *Rocky III*. From there he went to television, where he became a good guy and one of the stars of the very popular TV series "The A-Team." The man, of course, is Mr. T, a rough, tough former bodyguard who has become one of the most recognizable show business personalities in the land.

Mr. T is also a wrestling fan, and a personal friend of World Wrestling Federation champion Hulk Hogan. The two met on the set of *Rocky III,* where the Hulk portrayed a wrestler named Thunderlips. After that, Mr. T became a regular at many of the Hulk's matches. It was his presence at an early 1985 match, when the Hulk defended his title against Rowdy Roddy Piper, that may have changed the course of professional wrestling forever.

The Piper-Hogan encounter figured to be a bitter and

brutal battle. Rowdy Roddy was one of the most hated wrestlers on the scene, a guy who created as many enemies with his mouth as he did with his antics in the ring. Using his talk show, "Piper's Pit," as a forum, Rowdy Roddy insulted everyone in sight. Then, in December of 1984, Piper did something that really made him public enemy number one.

There was a huge wrestling show in New York, with more than 20,000 fans in attendance and millions more watching on cable TV. As part of the program, rock star and wrestling fan Cyndi Lauper was to be given a special award, a gold record for one of her big hits. In the midst of the presentation, Piper appeared. Professing to hate rock and roll music, Rowdy Roddy smashed the gold record over Lou Albano's head, then kicked Lauper clear across the ring. Captain Lou, of course, is a former wrestler and current manager who was also Lauper's friend and had appeared in several of her rock videos.

Piper had completely ruined the award ceremony and in doing so angered the Hulk, who immediately set the wheels in motion for their big, showdown battle. Piper made the most of the occasion, entering the ring accompanied by a twenty-piece bagpipe band, all the members wearing kilts, Piper's trademark. Rowdy Roddy again expressed his disgust for rock and roll and waited for the Hulk.

As the champ entered the ring, he stopped for a second by the front row to greet an old friend. Mr. T was in the audience and the two embraced as the crowd cheered wildly. Then the Hulk entered the ring to take care of Mr. Piper in a match dubbed "The War to Settle the Score."

In reality, however, it was just the beginning. The match was brutal, with more punching and gouging than actual wrestling. Each took turns meting out punishment to the other. But the tide turned for the villainous Piper when he began using a choke hold, then a sleeper that quickly became a choke. It weakened the Hulk, who managed to throw Roddy off, but the champ was still groggy.

That's when everything got out of hand. First Piper's crony, Cowboy Bob Orton, climbed up on the ring apron and tried to belt the Hulk with the cast on his broken arm. But the big man turned the tables and slammed Orton's arm into the ring post. Then the champ turned back to Piper and began working him over with forearm smashes. But one of them accidentally caught the referee and he went out cold.

Then Piper got some more unexpected help. Paul "Mr. Wonderful" Orndorff appeared in the ring, climbed to the top rope, and leaped knees first onto the Hulk's back. The champ went down . . . and out! Then both Piper and Orndorff began kicking the Hulk, as the fans gasped in horror. It looked as if their hero could be seriously injured, or worse.

The next unexpected appearance in the ring was from Cyndi Lauper. The little rock star got up on the ring apron and began screaming at Piper and Orndorff. They stopped pounding the Hulk and turned their attention to Lauper. First they knocked the rock star's hat off, and the horrified crowd wondered if the two bullies were about to injure the performer of "Girls Just Wanna Have Fun." It didn't look as if Lauper was having fun now.

Suddenly the 20,000 fans at Madison Square Garden let out a huge roar. The figure of Mr. T came leaping over the ropes and into the ring. The popular television hero quickly rescued Cyndi Lauper to a rousing cheer from the fans, but when he turned his back, Piper and Orndorff jumped him, knocking him to the canvas and stomping him. By then some thirty New York policemen were in the ring, trying to restore order. When Orndorff and Piper saw the Hulk regaining his feet, they beat a hasty retreat to the safety of the locker room. The match, or what it had become, was over.

Now both Hulk Hogan and Mr. T stood in the center of the ring, hands held high, the fans cheering, and they challenged both Piper and Orndorff to return to the ring. But the villains would have no part of that. Right then and there, Mr. T offered to team with the Hulk and pay back the dirty duo who had done them wrong.

"I like to see good, hard, clean wrestling," Mr. T said, "not the cowardly, dirty stuff. That's what it was when the two of them jumped the Hulk and went after Cyndi. From now on, whenever the Hulk needs me I'll be there, because he's the greatest wrestler there ever was."

Hulk Hogan was even angrier. "Piper is trying to destroy everything I stand for," he said. "What he did

WWF champ Hulk Hogan and TV star Mr. T salute each other and their fans after Mr. T helped rescue the Hulk from the clutches of Rowdy Roddy Piper, Bob Orton, and Paul Orndorff.

tonight calls for guerrilla warfare. I don't care what it takes, but Piper, Orndorff, and Orton will get it. They are three rats in a pack."

So the stage was set for more. The big match in the Garden had not only aroused the emotions of the fans, but it did a lot more for the sport of wrestling. It merged wrestling with both the music and show business industries. The Hulk was big-time now, and Mr. T vowed to wrestle with him against Piper and Orndorff. That would be an event to remember.

THE BRAWL TO SETTLE IT ALL

The sequel—called Wrestlemania—may have been the most amazing wrestling show ever. It took place March 31, 1985, in Madison Square Garden before a packed house of more than 22,500 fans. The card was also beamed through some 200 closed-circuit theaters throughout the United States and in five foreign countries. While the feature match was the eagerly awaited brawl between the team of Hulk Hogan and Mr. T versus Rowdy Roddy Piper and Paul "Mr. Wonderful" Orndorff, there were many other top-flight matches on the agenda.

It was a celebrity night, all right. The special ring announcer for the main event was New York Yankees manager Billy Martin, who is noted for a few brawls himself. And a guest referee was none other than Muhammad Ali, who needs no introduction. While the preliminary matches were exciting and action-packed, everyone was waiting for the main event, the Brawl to Settle It All!

Finally the time arrived. Piper, Orndorff, and the ever-present Orton entered first. Then, as "Eye of the Tiger" blared out of the loudspeakers, the Hulk and Mr. T entered the ring to a thunderous ovation. They were accompanied by another popular grappler, Jimmy "Superfly" Snuka, who was there just to help keep order.

As expected, the match began heatedly. Several times in the opening minutes all four combatants were in the ring at once and had to be restrained by the refs. It was obvious that there was no love lost between the two teams. But the huge crowd was loving it, already adopting Mr. T as one of their own, and chanting, "T . . . T . . . T . . . T" whenever he entered the ring.

The TV star was holding his own, especially for someone who hadn't wrestled professionally before. At one point, the evil Piper began working him over, but suddenly Mr. T punched Rowdy Roddy in the midsection, then hoisted him up, spun him around, and slammed him to the mat. And he looked like a seasoned pro doing it.

During another point in the match, Piper made the mistake of taking a swipe at Muhammad Ali. The former heavyweight champ immediately went into his boxing stance and drove Piper out of the ring with a series of quick left jabs. After that, Piper and Orndorff said they had had enough, that everyone was against

Mr. T hoists Roddy Piper to his shoulders as Hulk Hogan celebrates in the background during the Brawl to Settle It All.

them. They started leaving the ring and heading for the dressing room.

Referee Pat Patterson began counting. If they didn't return to the ring they would be disqualified. But no one, especially the Hulk and Mr. T, wanted the match to end like that. The champ then pinned the ref's arms to his sides, so he couldn't continue the count. He then blared out a challenge for Piper and Orndorff to return to the ring. Piper sneered, and the two returned. But as soon as they came back the Hulk grabbed them both and slammed their heads together as the crowd roared its approval.

The match reached its thrilling conclusion just minutes later. Orndorff and the Hulk were in there, but somehow Piper and Mr. T joined them and the four were again mixing it up. Orndorff had the Hulk in a full nelson when Cowboy Bob Orton decided to get into the act. He climbed the ring ropes and leaped off, intent on clobbering the Hulk with the cast on his broken arm.

But at the last second Hulk spun around and it was Orndorff who was belted by the plaster of Paris. Mr. Wonderful collapsed onto the mat and the Hulk quickly covered him. A three count and it was over. Hulk Hogan and Mr. T had done it! And to show their loyalty to a friend, Orton and Piper ran from the ring, leaving Paul Orndorff, still dazed, behind to face the victorious gladiators.

It had been a truly amazing night. Though a former bodyguard and rugged individual, Mr. T had never

The Hulk and Mr. T embrace after their great Wrestlemania
victory. The triumph of good over evil helped make professional wrestling more popular than ever.

wrestled before. Yet he had teamed with the great Hulk Hogan to defeat two of the best in the business. Stories of the match were all over the papers all across the country. Wrestling had become a media event. The Hulk and Mr. T, aided by Cyndi Lauper and all the special guest stars, had made Wrestlemania a night to remember.

BILL WATTS'S SNEAK ATTACK

One of the most shocking events in the history of professional wrestling took place back in 1965. On this very strangest of nights, the great World Wrestling Federation champion Bruno Sammartino was wrestling in a tag-team match against Slasher Sloan and the Golden Terror. His partner was a young wrestler named Bill Watts, and the two formed one of the most popular tag teams in the country.

Sammartino, of course, was already a beloved champion, dispatching many an evil villain to the delight of his legion of followers. Watts had come on the scene a year or so earlier, a big, 6'5" cowboy with a baby face and a quick smile. The fans took to him immediately, making him one of the most popular grapplers on the circuit. When Sammartino announced that he and Watts would be teaming up, there were sellout crowds waiting to see them at every turn.

Then came the match against Sloan and the Terror

and the strange turn of events that is difficult to explain even to this day. The Sammartino-Watts duo was having very little difficulty and the outcome of the match wasn't really in doubt. The fans at ringside were fully enjoying the action, figuring a pin was coming soon.

Sammartino, who was in the ring, decided it was time to get his partner into the action. He went over toward the corner and held out his hand for his partner to tag it. But instead of a tag, he got something else . . . a forearm smash across the jaw! Every fan in the house gasped in disbelief. So did Sammartino. Then bam . . . it happened again! Bill Watts was hammering at the face of his partner, the great Bruno Sammartino. It looked as if he had gone berserk.

Stunned by what was happening and by the force of the blows, Bruno sank down to his knees. A few more shots and he would be out cold. And Watts was still hammering, seemingly intent on doing real damage to his erstwhile partner. Finally the referee intervened, and with some help from ringside officials, managed to pull Watts off. The champ was helped to the corner, where he was still in a daze.

When Watts left the ring he was greeted by a cascade of boos for the first time in his career. But in the dressing room he said he knew exactly what he was doing.

"I felt I was getting the short end of the stick in this partnership," he said. "So I decided he wasn't worth being my partner. I just bided my time and studied his moves. When he came over to tag me, I said, 'Let's see how tough you really are,' and I began hammering away. And now that this is done with, I want his belt."

Though Watts said that the move was planned and that he didn't regret it, he probably didn't expect the reaction he got. In the course of one night, the cheers changed to jeers. And they stayed that way. What's more, when he regained his senses, Bruno Sammartino became enraged. He wanted revenge and was ready to meet Watts on a one-to-one basis.

Whenever that happened, Sammartino would batter Watts, turning violent. In fact, on several occasions Bruno was disqualified, something very rare for him, indeed. One time he had the match won, but wouldn't stop battering his fallen opponent until the ref was forced to disqualify him. Yet Watts continued to stand by his actions.

"If I had to do it again, I wouldn't hesitate," he said. "I had to make a big bid as a challenger, and that's why it had to be done that way. I don't care what any fan thinks, either."

But it was a move no one would ever forget, a double-cross that shocked the wrestling world. And while Bill Watts claimed he didn't regret it, he certainly paid for it . . . especially each time he met Bruno Sammartino.

A VERY PRECIOUS PARTNER

There was a time when a wrestler came to work, got in the ring, and did his thing. Unless it was a tag team match, the gladiator came and went alone. There was no such thing as a manager coming in with him and more often than not wreaking some of his own havoc during the match. But today it's all different.

Managers are everywhere. Renowned molders of men, such as Captain Lou Albano, Freddie Blassie, Bobby "The Brain" Heenan, and Gary Hart are nearly as well known as the men they manage. But in the world of big-time wrestling, something new happens nearly every night. Instead of a manager, a few wrestlers began coming into the ring with a woman.

One of the first was "Gorgeous" Jimmy Garvin, who introduced a beautiful blonde named Precious as his personal "valet." Precious would enter the ring with Garvin and help him get ready, removing his bright sequined pants and cape. Then she would strut around

Gorgeous Jimmy Garvin poses with his "personal valet," Precious, before Garvin challenged Rick Martel for the AWA title.

the ring and brag about the wrestling abilities of "Gorgeous" Jimmy. During the match, Precious became a cheerleader, urging Garvin on and defaming his opponent.

Then came a night in March of 1985, when Garvin was challenging the popular Rick Martel for the American Wrestling Association Heavyweight championship at the Meadowlands Arena in New Jersey. It was not only a rugged match between the two men, but also a night in which a woman may have directly influenced the outcome of a title bout.

The two wrestlers were evenly matched to begin with. Though Garvin is known as something of a rulebreaker, he also has natural wrestling skills and the quickness to compete with a highly scientific wrestler like Martel. What the champ didn't expect was the contribution of Precious. From the outset of the match she was shouting—encouragement to Garvin, and discouragement to Martel. In fact, the champ claimed that the things she said to him were a lot less than ladylike.

Being a pro, Martel could have coped with the verbal abuse, unnerving as it might have been. But then something else happened. The champion was on the verge of pinning "Gorgeous" Jimmy when Precious suddenly leaped over the ropes and attacked him from behind, just enough to allow Garvin to escape the pin attempt.

Moments later it happened again. Then again. What was Martel to do? He wasn't the kind of guy to turn around and belt a lady, and a very pretty one at that. But he also knew that it was possible to lose the

Gorgeous Jimmy proved a worthy opponent for champ Martel, and when he found himself in trouble he had Precious to bail him out. She attacked Martel on several occasions until he responded and was disqualified. Because there was no pin, however, Rick Martel retained his title.

match—and his title—because of this meddlesome woman.

Finally, Martel couldn't take it any longer. He tried to keep Precious out of the way by the best means he knew . . . and he wound up disqualified! It was unreal that the title match should end this way. Garvin and his Precious strutted around the ring, the winners, though the title remained with Rick Martel because it cannot change hands on a disqualification. But that didn't make the champion feel any better.

"I was disqualified for being ungentlemanly to a lady," he said afterward. "Can you top that one? Whenever I caught up with that weasel Garvin, that blond-haired maniac would scream at me. I've been around and I never heard a lady use language like that.

"But that wasn't the worst part. Every time I almost had him pinned, she came into the ring and attacked me. She must have jumped on me at least six times during the match. And *I* was disqualified!"

Rick Martel soon began a crusade to have women banned from working the corners during matches. "Gorgeous" Jimmy Garvin would never agree. His female valet is certainly an asset, and certainly aptly named. In fact, during his match with Rick Martel, she turned out to be the most precious ally he could hope to have.

YOUR HEAD OR MINE?

One of the most hated managers in the sport of wrestling today is Gary Hart. By contrast, one of the most beloved wrestling families today is the Von Erichs, Papa Fritz and his grappling sons, Kerry, Kevin, and Mike. When the two appear on opposite sides of the ring, it doesn't take long for the fireworks to start.

The Von Erichs always put on a huge show in their home state of Texas in memory of another son, David, who had died. It was the second annual David Von Erich Memorial Parade of Champions on May 5, 1985, at Texas Stadium, that really saw the Von Erich–Gary Hart feud come to a head—literally.

Hart was managing a mammoth, 468-pound wrestler aptly named One Man Gang. He figured the Gang was just the man to take apart one of the von Erichs, and he decided to challenge them before their home fans. It didn't take long for Fritz Von Erich to accept. He saw this as a chance to go one up on his longtime nemesis.

His son Kevin was meeting Ric Flair for the NWA title, so Papa Fritz decided to send son Kerry against the One Man Gang.

So the match was made. But it wasn't an ordinary matchup. There was a strange clause put into the contract. If One Man Gang won the match, then the Gang and manager Hart would have five minutes in the ring with Fritz Von Erich, himself a former wrestler. But if Kerry Von Erich emerged the winner, the Von Erichs would have the pleasure of shaving Gary Hart's head bald in front of 30,000 fans. And during the course of the match, Gary Hart and Fritz Von Erich would be handcuffed to each other, so neither could escape his punishment at the end of the contest.

Kerry Von Erich is like Samson, with long flowing hair and a perfectly developed, muscular, 260-pound body. He is a former NWA champ and one of the strongest wrestlers in the world. With his father's pride and possibly good health at stake, he was not about to let One Man Gang take control of the match.

Early in the match Kerry got the Gang in a headlock and showed he could match the giant strength for strength. He continued to dominate the match, putting the Gang in a painful claw hold as Fritz Von Erich smiled and Gary Hart appeared nervous. He didn't want his head shaved in front of all those screaming Texans.

So several minutes later, as Kerry started to lift the One Man Gang for a bodyslam, Gart Hart managed to reach into the ring and trip Kerry Von Erich. That

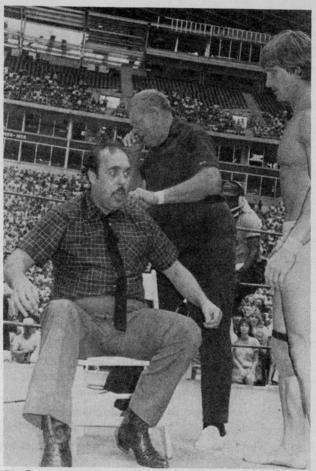

The strange end to the match between Kerry Von Erich and One Man Gang. After Von Erich won, his father-manager, Fritz Von Erich, collected on a bet by shaving the head of One Man Gang's manager, Gary Hart.

started it. Papa Fritz, handcuffed to Hart, began beating on the manager, and in the ring, One Man Gang took advantage of the unexpected help to slam Kerry to the mat.

Now the giant moved toward the ropes to get ready for the big splash. And with 468 pounds behind him, the Gang could deliver a splash that would bury any opponent. Only this time Fritz Von Erich paid back Hart. He tripped up the One Man Gang and gave his son a chance to escape. Kerry quickly turned the match back around and got the pin. He was the winner.

With 30,000 fans screaming and cheering, the Von Erichs went to work. First they uncuffed Fritz and Hart. Then, while one of them held the manager, the other managed to handcuff One Man Gang to the ring post, so he wouldn't interfere. Then they turned back to Hart.

The fans roared as the Von Erich boys held the struggling manager while Papa Fritz got a pair of electric clippers and went to work. Slowly he shaved the manager's head as the crowd roared. The One Man Gang was going berserk, trying to escape the cuffs to help Hart. He slowly dismantled the entire ring post, but by the time he got free it was too late. Gary Hart had been shaved bald. Hopefully, he had learned a lesson. When you mess around with the Von Erichs in Texas, you're looking for trouble. It could even cost you every hair on your head!

AS BIG AS A HAYSTACK...
OR BIGGER

Would you believe there was a professional wrestler who weighed 625 pounds? His name was Haystack Calhoun, and while he wrestled successfully during the 1950s and 1960s, his biggest battle was convincing people that he was a legitimate athlete, not some oversized freak. Of course, that wasn't always easy to do when fans saw him win matches by simply sitting on opponents and crushing them.

Haystack weighed nearly 12 pounds at birth, and went on from there. His father weighed 230 pounds and his mother 135. But he had an Aunt Cara who tipped the scales at 510 and she's the one Haystack took after. By the time he was 15 he weighed 385, and when he turned 19, he had reached 500 pounds. And he was still a growing boy.

When he first decided to try wrestling, several trainers and promoters sent him packing. They, too, felt he had too much size and couldn't be effective. But Haystack had played high school football and could move as fast as much smaller players. Finally he met a former wrestling champ named Orville Brown, who decided to give the youngster a chance. But Brown also knew that the big kid would have to be promoted right.

"I can't present you like just some ordinary wrestler," he told him. "You just aren't built ordinary. What I'd want to do is make you a farm-boy wrestler. You'll grow whiskers, put on overalls and I'll call you Country Boy Calhoun."

So that's how it started. William D. Calhoun became Country Boy, and later Haystack, when someone in the audience hollered that he was as big as a haystack. And he fought against the best, claiming that Bruno Sammartino was the strongest man he ever met and the only one to ever take him off his feet.

Big as he is, Haystack suffered his share of injuries, including broken ribs, a slipped disc in his back and muscle spasms in his neck and shoulders. And because of his immense size, he hurt his ankles numerous times. For the record, he had a 68-inch waist, 54-inch thighs, 24-inch biceps and a 24-inch neck.

Fortunately for his opponents, Haystack was basically easygoing. Otherwise, many of the men who wrestled him might have been hurt. Haystack didn't like hurting people. He just wanted to win matches and convince people he wasn't a freak. In fact, he was a hard-working athlete who took good care of himself. The 625 pounds were just his natural weight.

"I don't gorge myself on food," said Haystack. "I

eat sensibly and not much before a match. My main meal comes afterward. Doctors who have examined me have said I'm doing the right thing. I'm a big man, but there's nothing wrong with me."

But there are special needs for a man so large. When he travels by air, Haystack has to buy two plane tickets because he takes up both halves of a double seat. He owns a specially made station wagon built on a pickup truck frame with extra-heavy-duty shocks and springs. Because he broke so many beds in hotel rooms, he took to sleeping on the floor.

Yet maybe the strangest thing that happened because of his weight was the time in Boston when he caused an elevator to snap its cables and fall to the bottom.

"I think the elevator girl got so scared when I got on that she forgot to push the stop button. We hit the bottom pretty hard and it was kinda scary."

Haystack Calhoun often faced two or three men at a time during his career. That evened the odds a bit, though he still emerged victorious most of the time. Yet there was a time when he met a man bigger than he was. And that's still another story.

THE SAD SAGA
OF HAPPY HUMPHREY

The one man Haystack Calhoun wrestled who was bigger than he was William Cobb, professionally known as Happy Humphrey. Unbelievable as it may be, Happy Humphrey wrestled at a weight that sometimes exceeded 800 pounds. Even Haystack must have felt small alongside this largest of all men. But there was a difference, as Haystack mentioned some time after their match.

"When I wrestled Happy he weighed about 700 pounds," Haystack said. "But I could see as soon as we squared off that he was a fat 700. He had very poor balance and he was easy to move around and handle. I slammed him easier than the average-size fellow. When I learned he had gone up to 800 pounds I warned him it wasn't healthy."

As it turned out, Haystack Calhoun was right. But backtracking a bit, it's not hard to see why Happy Humphrey became a professional wrestler. It seemed a natural after he lasted 28 minutes with a 600-pound bear!

That happened back in 1954. Happy was a big twenty-six-year-old then. He's always been big, weighing 18 pounds at birth and passing the 300-pound mark by the time he was twelve.

"I could out-eat two men back then," he remembered.

By the time he was a teenager, Happy had the strength to match his weight, and could carry a 500-pound bale of cotton on his back. So by the time the guy with the bear stopped in Macon, Georgia, with his challenge, Happy Humphrey was ready. The deal was that the promoter would pay a certain amount of money for each minute a man could stay in there with the seven-foot bear known as Big Ginger.

Young Happy astounded everyone by lasting 28 minutes. For his Herculean effort he was paid the grand sum of $200. But it got him to thinking about wrestling, and pretty soon he was out touring around. By 1956 he had turned professional. For a few years his career was in high gear. In Oklahoma City he met and defeated eleven top wrestlers, all at one time. Not too many survived Happy's "Squash," which simply meant the 800-pounder would sit on them.

Between 1956 and 1962 Happy wrestled all over the world, traveling about 90,000 miles a year. Like Haystack Calhoun, Happy often traveled in a specially made car.

"I had an old model Chrysler with big doors and an extra set of shock absorbers," he said. "Someone else always had to drive because I couldn't fit behind the steering wheel."

There were other places Happy couldn't fit, either. One time in Montgomery, Alabama, he went into a phone booth to make a call. That part went all right. It was when he turned to leave that things suddenly went sour. He couldn't get out. He was stuck tight in the booth. Someone called a cop, and they eventually had to get the telephone company out to take the booth apart.

Another time, in New Orleans, Happy went to the movies. He said he usually sat on the edge of the seat to avoid problems, but this time he became so absorbed in the movie that he relaxed and slowly sat back.

"Before I knew it I was wedged into the seat. It took seven cops to get me outta there. They had to cut the seats all around me and by the time they finished there were something like eight fire trucks outside and a whole crowd of people trying to figure out what was going on."

Happy could live with these mishaps as long as he was a top-flight grappler and felt all right. But in the early 1960s all that weight began to cause problems for him.

A number of years earlier he had undergone a surgical procedure to pare a hundred pounds off his immense frame. But he had put the weight back quickly.

Then in Oklahoma, in 1962, it all caught up with him. He was just thirty-four years old but suddenly he couldn't move without help.

"I needed a cane to walk," he said, "and I couldn't even get across a room without stopping to rest. I even needed help to get off my bed and move to the table."

Happy's lifestyle and legendary appetite had caught up with him. The man who had eaten fifteen fried chickens at one time, and eighteen pounds of fried catfish on another occasion, would never eat like that again if he wanted to live. Nor would he ever wrestle again.

To save his life, Happy Humphrey became a volunteer patient at the teaching hospital of the Medical College of Georgia, where he went on a carefully supervised diet. He would eat just one meal a day of just 1,000 calories. His goal was to get down to 240 pounds, which would make his total weight loss nearly 600 pounds. Incredible!

But Happy Humphrey worked at it, trying to make the best of an unhappy situation. His size 90 trousers were a thing of the past, and the weight came off, under the watchful eye of the doctors. Within two years, Happy made it. He was down to 230 pounds and able to resume a normal life. But he acknowledged that he'd always miss wrestling.

"Wrestling was good to me and I miss being in there and mixing it up," he said. "It's a sport for tough men and I loved it."

So William Cobb, a.k.a. Happy Humphrey, would no longer be able to apply the squash to another wrestler. But the new Happy was able to do something that he had never before done in his life. He could sit in a chair and cross his legs.

NOW YOU SEE IT...

Back in the spring of 1963, the World Wrestling Federation champion was a fair-haired grappler named Buddy Rogers. His nickname, the Blond Devil, should tell you about his style in the ring. There were plenty of villains on the East Coast then, men like Killer Kowalski, the Crusher, Karl Von Hess, and Skull Murphy. But it was Buddy Rogers who got the fans' blood boiling the most.

The big question was, could anyone defeat Rogers? Some top-flight grapplers had tried, the likes of Eduardo Carpentier, Bobo Brazil, Kowalski, Buddy Dixon, and Dory Austin. None had been able to bring the Blond Devil to his knees. But there was a new challenge being mounted, by a strong young wrestler with impressive credentials. His name was Bruno Sammartino.

Sammartino came east that spring, was soundly defeating everyone he faced, and beginning to clamor for a shot at Buddy Rogers. At first Rogers stalled by claiming he had other contenders to meet and defeat. Then in mid-April, he gave the youngster a shot, but it was in a non-title bout. Rogers set the tone by attacking young Sammartino before the bell even sounded. He was hoping to intimidate the youngster and perhaps put an end to his title hopes right there.

But Bruno weathered the opening storm and eventually took control of the match with strength holds that weakened the Blond Devil. The bout was finally ruled no contest, but now the fans and the press wanted the two to meet for the title. It would be difficult for Rogers to stonewall again.

He tried, by saying he'd face Sammartino "when I'm good and ready." But the public clamor continued, and finally Rogers agreed to meet Bruno again, this time on May 17, at Madison Square Garden, with the WWF title at stake. When the day arrived, the old Garden was packed to the rafters, and almost every single fan in the arena was rooting for young Bruno Sammartino. But none had the faintest idea of what was about to happen.

When Rogers was introduced, he was soundly booed. Maybe that made him do it, or maybe he just forgot what had happened in their previous bout. But the champ figured if he attacked Sammartino quickly and viciously, using every rulebreaking trick in the book, the youngster might be intimidated and submit.

But Bruno was ready. He fended off the initial attack by the champ and began smashing at Rogers with his forearms. Then he dropkicked the Blond Devil to the canvas, then again, and again. From there he got him in a bearhug, his tremendous strength squeezing the breath right out of the champ.

Rogers was helpless, putty in the hands of the challenger. Almost without strain, the young Sammartino then lifted Rogers overhead and put him into the deadly backbreaker. Within seconds, Rogers had submitted. Sammartino deposited him on the canvas and walked away, the new WWF champion.

The fans went wild, screaming for their new idol. But it had happened so fast it was almost hard to believe. In fact, if you had gone out for a hot dog or soda, you would have missed it. Amazingly enough, Bruno Sammartino had defeated Buddy Rogers in a record-breaking 48 seconds!

AN INCREDIBLE
TAG TEAM

Tag teams are formed in many ways. Sometimes, two wrestlers have the same philosophy. Other times they might feel they complement each other, the strength of the one making up for the weakness of the other. Or they might just be close friends who want to team up in the ring. In some cases, two matmen might just feel they want to win a title, and working together is the best way to do it.

But perhaps the strangest coupling in wrestling history occurred when the popular Dusty Rhodes, known as the American Dream, chose the egotistical and fanciful Adrian Street for a tag-team partner. Not only did their wrestling philosophies and styles contrast, but the two grapplers did not really like each other. In fact, their feelings bordered on hate!

Then why in the world did these two team up? After all, Dusty Rhodes was one of the most popular wrestlers around, a former champion who had spent years on the circuit battling the likes of Adrian Street and other notorious rulebreakers. And Street, a prancing Englishman, whose outlandish hairstyle, clothing, and makeup had seen him dubbed the Boy George of the wrestling world, loved nothing better than to defeat the likes of Dusty Rhodes. So what gives?

Well, in truth, this Odd Couple of the tag-team world resulted from a feud, a desire for revenge. Chalk up another reason for new tag teams. And the idea belonged to Dusty Rhodes.

It seemed as if Dusty was in the midst of a feud with notorious rulebreakers Buzz Sawyer and Kevin Sullivan. More than anything, the American Dream wanted to defeat those two. But he wanted to do more than defeat them; he wanted to humiliate them and he thought of a unique way to do it.

"I wanted to prove I could beat those bums with any partner," Rhodes said. "I told them I could take a man I admire less than anyone and still run them out of the ring. So I wanted a partner who would serve as an insult to Sullivan and Sawyer."

That's how the American Dream came to choose Adrian Street. It couldn't have been very flattering to Street, especially when Dusty Rhodes didn't mince words about his partner-to-be.

"Adrian Street's prancing stupidity is enough to make me sick," he said. "I knew that by me teaming with him, Sullivan and Sawyer would consider it a slap in the face, and there's nothing a man hates more than a slap in the face. I know Street hates my guts as much as

I hate his, but the offer was crazy enough to appeal to someone who wears makeup and never goes anywhere without that Amazon valet of his."

Dusty Rhodes must have known his psychology. Street accepted and came to the match accompanied by his female valet, Miss Linda. The showdown was held in Orlando, Florida, and Dusty stood by calmly as Street and Miss Linda even sprayed the American Dream with some sort of sweet-smelling perfume, and the crowd ate it up.

By this time, Sawyer and Sullivan were enraged, something Rhodes was hoping would happen. He figured that enraged wrestlers make mistakes, and he was right. Their anger led to recklessness and Rhodes managed to take advantage of it. He dominated the match, to the point where he didn't even allow Street to see much action. When the match ended, Sawyer and Sullivan were soundly beaten—not really by the Odd Couple, for they were beaten mostly by Dusty Rhodes.

But Sawyer and Sullivan weren't the only ones angered by the result of the match. The Odd Couple was about to split. Adrian Street realized that he was little more than window dressing for Rhodes, a setup used to anger their opponents so that Rhodes could take his revenge. To regain a little of his lost pride, Street immediately challenged Dusty to a match where they would be on opposite sides of the ring.

Now Rhodes figured he could show his former partner what he really thought of him. But Street attacked with a fury, quickly showing the Dream he was more

The fanciful Adrian Street, with his valet, Miss Linda, prances toward the ring before teaming with Dusty Rhodes in a tag-team match. It was an Odd Couple combination, all right. Later, Street and Rhodes battled against each other with uncompromising fury.

than a prancer and a dancer. He was also a dangerous wrestler. The bout deteriorated into a bloody war, and ended when the referee disqualified both men.

After the match Rhodes admitted he now had more respect for Adrian Street as a wrestler, but added that he never again would team with him under any circumstances. Then he thought a minute, and said:

"But I guess anything can happen in wrestling."

That's the truth, all right. After all, if anyone had predicted that Dusty Rhodes and Adrian Street would be tag-team partners, he would have been rushed off to the funny farm. But it happened, one of the strangest and most incredible ring events in recent years.

DON'T MESS
WITH THE BRUISER

It seems like there was always a connection between Dick the Bruiser and football. Maybe that's because he started out as a football player, but when he gave that up for his work in the squared circle, he seemed to have a lingering need to prove something to those in the gridiron world.

In the late 1940s, Richard Afflis was a high school football star, then an all–Big Ten selection as a sophomore at Purdue. From there he transferred to the University of Nevada, where he became an all-Pacific tackle. The Green Bay Packers of the National Football League drafted him, and he played guard for the Pack from 1951 to 1955. The last two years he was the club's offensive captain.

The story has it that San Francisco 49er defensive tackle Leo Nomellini first encouraged Afflis to become a wrestler. Nomellini was a part-time grappler during his tenure in the NFL and, playing opposite Dick Afflis, was impressed by his strength, quickness, and courage, all qualities that would be helpful in the ring.

But there was one thing that Nomellini didn't see. That was the meanness. For once Richard Afflis made his commitment to wrestling, he became Dick the Bruiser, a six-foot, 250-pound terror who struck fear in the hearts of opponents everywhere.

It wasn't long before Dick the Bruiser had risen to the top of another profession. His crewcut, square-jawed countenance wasn't frightening in itself. But the fury he unleashed in the ring was.

"There isn't a man alive I can't lick," the Bruiser said on many occasions. "No man I've ever wrestled has convinced me I couldn't lick him. It seems like the only way I lose is on disqualifications."

Before matches, the Bruiser would work himself into a fury. One night, while he was in the locker room getting psyched, he heard a lot of laughter and cheering coming from the arena. It seems that a good-looking female fan was doing a wild dance that was really entertaining the crowd. Suddenly the Bruiser charged out of his dressing room like an enraged bull.

"Get that dame outta here!" he roared. "The Bruiser is wrestling here tonight and I don't want this bunch of yaks getting in a happy mood." Sure enough, ring officials told the girl to stop. No one was about to mess with the Bruiser.

There was even a time he whipped 20,000 fans at New York's Madison Square Garden into a riotous frenzy with his antics. Some three hundred people were injured that night, but the Bruiser just laughed it off.

But perhaps the strangest incident of the Bruiser's career occurred in 1963. Once again, his toughness brought him national headlines. The Bruiser was wrestling in Detroit, and one evening he entered a bar run by Alex Karras, the all-pro defensive tackle of the Detroit Lions. Karras wasn't playing football in 1963. He was serving a one-year suspension for an infraction of NFL rules.

With Dick the Bruiser in the bar, things didn't stay calm for long. First, the Bruiser challenged Karras to a wrestling match, and the big tackle accepted. But before he left, the Bruiser ended up in a battle with eight of the bar's customers and it took police to break up the wild melée.

Sure enough, Karras followed through and the match was held at the Detroit Olympia before some 16,000 fans. It was a real brawl, with the 260-pound Karras giving the Bruiser all he could handle. But in the end, experience told the story and the Bruiser won.

It wasn't the end of it, though. Karras wanted more, and the two fought a series of matches throughout the Midwest. Their bouts were both popular and profitable, and while the Bruiser came out on top, Karras proved to be more than a worthy opponent.

Why the strange challenge? Maybe the Bruiser wanted to prove that he had gone into an even rougher sport than football. Perhaps there were some whispers that he was a quitter because he left the NFL for the squared circle. What's certain is that the Bruiser went into Karras's bar looking for a fight, and he found one.

But then again Dick the Bruiser was always looking for a fight. He backed down from no man and was ready to wreak his personal brand of mayhem wherever he went. Mention the name of Dick the Bruiser, and fans knew they would get their money's worth. For with the Bruiser, every bout was tantamount to war.

THE LEGEND OF HATPIN MARY

In the early 1950s, television was still a relatively new thing. The first superstar of the small screen was the man they called Mr. Television, comedian Milton Berle. But another early star of the boob tube was professional wrestling. Fans could catch ring action on several different channels several times a week.

The telecasts were not nearly as colorful as they are today, and one channel even used to crinkle paper into the microphone to simulate bones breaking from a tough hold. It wasn't very effective. But the wrestling was good, with such veterans as Gorgeous George, Don the Magnificent, Les Ruffin, Gene Stanley, and the Golden Superman.

There was another permanent fixture on those early wrestling telecasts. Seated at ringside, always in the first row, was a little old lady, a grandmotherly type, who you might expect would be home baking cookies. Maybe she baked the cookies by day, but at night she was always at Sunnyside Gardens or St. Nicholas Arena, or even Madison Square Garden, wherever there was a wrestling card in New York City.

During the matches this little lady with the eye-glasses and omnipresent hat on her head showed little emotion. She sat and watched . . . that is, until the wrestlers arrived in front of her. You see, this elderly woman didn't like villains, the men they call rulebreakers today. And when they were close enough for her to reach them, she sprang into action.

She would reach up to the hat she always wore and remove from it another anachronism of days gone by: the hatpin. Women used to use long pins to hold hats on their heads, and this lady always carried one. What she did with the hatpin would probably make some of today's rulebreakers proud. She would go to work on the wrestler she didn't like. Needless to say, he didn't stay in that place long.

No one knew her real name. But to everyone in attendance and those watching on television, she became known as Hatpin Mary. Even the announcers would be watching when the grapplers got close. "Watch it, he's too close to Hatpin Mary." Or, "Here comes Hatpin Mary." For a while, there were even imitators appearing at arenas outside the city.

It wasn't a golden age of wrestling for sure. But it had its heroes, its moments, and its characters. One of the funniest and strangest, without a doubt, had to be that little lady known as Hatpin Mary.

went at it for several minutes, both in and out of the ring, before order could be restored.

But while the two were separated, they continued to taunt and shout at each other. They were still at it when the bell rang signaling the third fall. It's doubtful Blassie even heard it, so intent on insulting Graham was he. But Thesz did. He raced across the ring and bombed Freddie with a flying dropkick. That was the beginning of the end for Freddie Blassie. Thesz continued to work him over and within minutes had him pinned to take the match.

Blassie was enraged. He was like a wild man, yelling at everyone and even attacking the referee. When he spotted Eddie Graham again he placed the blame for his loss on the other wrestler.

"It's your fault I lost this match," he bellowed. "I had the guy beat. Now I'm gonna tear you apart."

It took several ring officials and auxiliary police to keep the two grapplers apart. It wasn't long after, however, that Blassie started all over again, proclaiming to be the real champ and that he was robbed, and that he would take care of Eddie Graham, Lou Thesz, and anyone else who wanted *his* title.

That was Freddie Blassie, all right. Oddly enough, though, part of what he said was true. He was very close to beating Thesz. Ringside observers saw how weak and shaky the champ seemed after the second fall. If only Blassie hadn't been distracted by Eddie Graham. If only he had kept his cool and concentrated on the match. If only . . .

But he wouldn't have been Freddie Blassie if he did. Like many wrestlers who claim they are the greatest, they often prove their own worst enemy. Blassie had the title within his grasp and, because of a strange turn of events, let it slip away.

HYPE OR TRIPE?

Most people who followed the rise of the World Wrestling Federation as an East Coast phenomenon in the mid-1980s have attributed its popularity to one man: the huge, charismatic champion Hulk Hogan. And indeed the Hulkster may be the most recognizable grappler of his era. Perhaps even its wealthiest, with all the commercial spinoffs on his name and reputation.

But there are those insiders who say the WWF would never have attained its mass appeal had it not been for one Rowdy Roddy Piper. What! Roddy Piper? Wait a minute. Isn't he the WWF's resident villain, one of the most hated men in wrestling? Yes, that's true. And while it sounds incredible at first, the entire rise of the WWF as a real wrestling superpower may have been orchestrated by Rowdy Roddy with a little help from his friends.

Though it may come as a surprise to some, Roddy Piper's background in wrestling is extensive. This native of Glasgow, Scotland, began wrestling at the age of six. By the time he was 16 he was beginning his pro career in Canada. And within four years he became the lightweight champion of the world. He was the youngest wrestler ever to achieve that honor. Legitimate credentials, to be sure.

Yet when Roddy Piper arrived on the WWF scene in 1983, he was not an active grappler. Strange as it may seem, the Rowdy one was mainly a manager, handling "Mr. Wonderful," Paul Orndorff, and "Mr. D," David Shultz. The only noise Piper made then was with his mouth. And boy was he good at that, so good that it wasn't long before he was asked to host his own interview show within the WWF telecasts. It was aptly called "Piper's Pit," and it proved a springboard for Piper and the WWF.

For those who know the recent history of the WWF, and even for those who are more general wrestling fans, the list of Rowdy Roddy's actions from the "Pit" have laid the groundwork for much of the WWF action that has taken place since his arrival.

1. He began feuds with such good-guy wrestlers as Jimmy "Superfly" Snuka, Tony Atlas, Sergeant Slaughter, Hulk Hogan, and Andre the Giant.

2. He expressed his disdain for rock star Cyndi Lauper, who was an avowed wrestling freak and manager of women's champ Wendi Richter.

3. He found proof to dispute claims by Captain Lou Albano that Albano had helped write some of

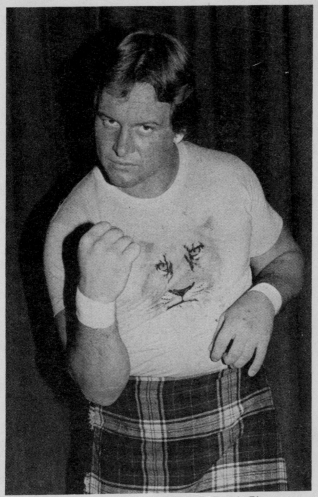
The man everyone loves to hate, Rowdy Roddy Piper.

Ms. Lauper's hit songs and was the mastermind behind Lauper's career. This precipitated a temporary feud between Albano and Cyndi Lauper.

4. He found a way to infuriate television personality Mr. T, drawing him into the ring and prompting him to get directly involved in ring combat as a tag-team partner with Hulk Hogan. The champ, by the way, also despises Piper.

5. He disrupted a gold record presentation to Cyndi Lauper by seizing the record and smashing it over the head of Captain Lou Albano, then claiming he hated rock and roll. This further infuriated Hulk Hogan and Mr. T.

6. Because of all the feuds and hatreds he created, Piper became the top attraction at the big Wrestlemania show in 1985, which featured a tag-team match between Piper and Paul Orndorff, Hulk Hogan, and Mr. T. It was one of the most successful wrestling promotions of all time.

So the list of Rowdy Roddy's dubious, but effective, achievements continues to grow. He's been voted the most hated wrestler in the WWF, but the fans flock to see him perform. And with his incredible gift of gab and the forum of the "Pit," Roddy Piper has emerged as a wrestling phenomenon and a household name. His ability inside the squared circle has always been suspect, but if you let him start talking, watch out!

LIKE FATHER, UNLIKE SON

Most fathers can't be any prouder than to have a son follow in their footsteps. And most sons who do follow in their fathers' footsteps are equally proud of their dads' accomplishments. But leave it to the world of professional wrestling to produce its own unusual version of fathers and sons.

Of course, there are some standard relationships. David Sammartino is now carrying on the family name for his retired champion father, Bruno. Angelo Mosca, Jr., joined the ring wars while Angelo, Sr., continued to grapple. They even use the same name. Mike Graham makes no secret that his father is the legendary Eddie Graham.

But then there's Blackjack Mulligan, Sr., and Blackjack Mulligan, Jr. Wait a minute! You say you never heard of Blackjack Mulligan, Jr.? And you can't remember Blackjack Mulligan using "Sr." after his name? Well, you're right. There is no Blackjack

Mulligan, Jr., at least not registered with any of the wrestling federations. You see, Blackjack Mulligan's son wrestles under the name Barry Windham!

It's one of the strangest father-son relationships in all of sport. Barry Windham apparently wanted to make it on his own. He didn't want to float in on anyone's coattails. And perhaps it's even more important that his style was distinctly different from that of his father.

Blackjack is a brawler, a rough, tough veteran who knows every trick in the book and can rumble with the best of them. Barry Windham, on the other hand, is a scientific wrestler who rarely breaks the rules, or at least that's how he started out. But after capturing the Florida heavyweight title and the Southern heavyweight championship, Barry was injured in an auto accident and had to give up his titles.

When he recovered and could wrestle again, Barry decided to mend some fences. He took a new tag-team partner. His name: Blackjack Mulligan. At first, the father didn't think it was a good idea.

"I'm the type of wrestler who attracts enemies," Blackjack said. "Why should Barry inherit my enemies? They're my problem, not his."

Barry Windham disagreed. He said the same kind of guys would come after him sooner or later, whether it was to get revenge on Blackjack or not. "I've got my own reputation," he said. "And I'm at the point where I attract top rulebreakers. I'm on my own now and being your son isn't my only claim to fame."

So father and son joined forces and became an effective team, winning a number of titles down South. The partnership was especially profitable for Barry Windham. He learned a great deal from his more experienced father and it made him a more resourceful wrestler. Now he was ready to handle any kind of attack and to better deal with the rulebreakers.

But in the fragile world of wrestling, egos can do strange things. Soon father and son had a falling out and a parting of the ways. Before long, new fans once again had no idea that Barry Windham was Blackjack Mulligan's son. In fact, the few times they were in the same area, there was always someone suggesting the two meet. After all, fans always love to see a tough, grizzled veteran meet a scientific, clean-cut youngster. Of course, that never happened.

Barry was right about one thing. He was making enemies on his own. He returned to Florida and recaptured the Southern heavyweight title. That's when a feud developed between young Windham and the rulebreaking grapplers managed by the devious J. J. Dillon. Barry had to cope with the likes of Angelo Mosca, Sr., The Purple Haze, Frank Dusek, and Kevin Sullivan.

Seeing the problems his son was having, Blackjack decided to bury the hatchet once more. Seems as if the blood bond between the two was stronger than their different ring philosophies and respective egos. So Blackjack came south and brought with him his good friend Dusty Rhodes. Joining Windham, the three waged war against Dillon's forces in a series of extremely rough-and-tumble matches.

When the two parted again, it was not only as father and son, but as friends, each willing to help the other whenever help was needed. So this strangest of father-son relationships continues. Now it is one of mutual respect. Maybe it had to be this way, for Barry Windham was able to get out of his father's shadow early, forge his own way with his own style, and make it on his own.

The popular and powerful Kerry Von Erich.

THE ONE AND ONLY ROCCA

Wrestling fans today are used to seeing their favorites flying around the ring. When a barefooted Jimmy "Superfly" Snuka climbs onto the top of the ring posts and flies through the air, the fans gasp with the electricity of the moment. It's almost incredible to see such a big, muscular man perform almost unbelievable ring acrobatics.

But it had to come from somewhere. After all, there was a time when wrestlers stayed pretty much in the center of the ring, locking horns in mortal combat. That was before Antonino Rocca came on the scene in the late 1940s. Rocca was a native of Italy who had grown up in Argentina. He was the first significant wrestler to enter the ring barefooted, and it didn't take fans and opponents long to find out why.

Rocca wrestled as much with his feet and legs as with his arms. He bounced around the ring like a gazelle, often doing handstands and swatting his opponents with a foot. He was an acrobat, a high flyer who used the ring ropes as a launching pad to clobber his opponents. His flying drop-kick was a sight to behold, and bigger, stronger men were dazzled by Rocca's high-flying tactics.

In the 1950s, when pro wrestling was often on television, Rocca was the main attraction. One promoter claimed that with the exception of Mr. Television, Milton Berle, Antonino Rocca sold more television sets in the 1950s than any other personality. Wrestling fans all across the country knew that to be held in the "Argentine Backbreaker" meant the match was over and Rocca was the winner again.

Rocca retired in 1968 and returned to Argentina. But in 1975 he returned to the U.S. as a commentator and once again felt the lure of the ring. He got together with his old tag-team partner, Miguel Perez, and the two surprised the wrestling world by winning the North American tag-team championship from the Infernos.

When the duo lost the title, Rocca retired again. On February 17, 1977, there was a night in his honor in New York as a grateful Rocca signed autographs and refereed the main event of the evening. He seemed genuinely happy that so many people remembered and loved him. Two days later, Rocca entered Roosevelt Hospital in New York, where shortly afterward a shocked wrestling world learned that he had died.

But all those who saw Rocca wrestle in the 1950s and '60s will never forget him. To them, the barefooted grappler from Argentina may have been the most incredible wrestler who ever lived.

GOOD GUYS, BAD GUYS, GOOD GUYS... GET IT STRAIGHT!

There have been a number of pro wrestlers who have switched horses in midstream. For one reason or another, they have gone from good to bad, or bad to good. But seldom do they switch back again. Yet there was once a wrestler who went from a popular hero, to a "maniac," and finally straightened out his act once more.

It's a storybook beginning. Once upon a time there was a clean-cut college wrestler at the University of Buffalo. As he contended in his amateur bouts at the University, he noticed there was a young boy at all his matches who seemed to admire him greatly. Don Curtis never forgot his young fan, and even thought about him occasionally after he began his professional career.

Big Don still had that clean-cut image as a pro. He was one of the good guys and always a crowd favorite. Several years after he turned pro, Don Curtis noticed a young wrestler who was also from Buffalo. The kid looked familiar. After a quick conversation, Don Curtis knew why. The youngster's name was Mark Lewin, and he was the same kid who used to watch Don so closely at the university.

The storybook tale continued. Don Curtis and Mark Lewin became fast friends, and before long they decided to team up. The result was one of the best tag-team combinations in wrestling, good enough to win the United States Tag-Team Championship.

Curtis and Lewin were the good guys, and heavy favorites whenever they met the resident villains. They could handle any kind of rulebreaking wrestlers, and their teamwork was a thing to behold. It got so that no one could think of Don Curtis without Mark Lewin, and vice versa. They were a team and they seemed inseparable.

But then the inevitable happened. Since nothing goes on forever, Don and Mark decided to split and try it on their own for a while. Time passed and Don was unfortunately injured in the ring. While he was recuperating, an old friend, another grappler, came by to visit him. The man had been wrestling in Texas and what he told Don Curtis shocked him into silence.

"Your old sidekick, Lewin, is really causing a stir down in Texas," the man said. "He's just about the most unpopular wrestler in the whole state. His nickname down there is 'Maniac' Mark Lewin."

Curtis was still in a depressed mood the next day when he had another visitor. To his great surprise, Mark Lewin walked in, looking much the same as he had when he left. He certainly didn't appear to be a maniac. He told Don that he had heard about his injury and wanted to help him settle the score with the men who did it, a tag team known as the Assassins.

But finally Don Curtis could contain himself no longer. He asked his former partner about the stories from Texas about "Maniac" Mark Lewin. Reluctantly, Mark Lewin admitted they were true. But what was it that changed an all-American boy into a maniac? Only the world of professional wrestling can do something like that.

It seems that after Lewin and Curtis split up, Mark went out on his own, and in Kansas City had a series of brutal matches with a chronic rulebreaker. Not only did he learn a slew of dirty tricks, he found himself badly injured with time to think. What he decided was that no one would treat him like that again, and he'd do whatever was necessary to prevent it.

Once he recovered and went to Texas, Lewin put his new theories into practice and was booed for the first time in his career. Then came a series of matches with local hero Cowboy Bob Ellis, a series that rapidly developed into a feud. Ellis was one of the most popular grapplers in the state. To the fans, he could do no wrong, and this drove Lewin to greater extremes. So by the time he was through with Ellis, the "Maniac" title had been put before his name.

Still Don Curtis believed in his old friend. He willingly accepted him as a partner again and the two went to work. When they met the Assassins, they gave the masked villains one of their worst beatings ever, and they did it without chronic rulebreaking. Working with Don Curtis again had taught Mark Lewin an invaluable lesson.

"I learned from the man I have always admired the most that it's possible to be injured deliberately and get back at the guys who did it, yet still remain a gentleman in the ring."

So Mark Lewin returned to Texas to settle some scores, but he didn't go back as the "Maniac." He was once again the wrestler he had been when he first teamed with Don Curtis to form one of the great tag teams of our time. And the good guy who had become a bad guy was a good guy once more in the often tangled, but always amazing world of wrestling.

IS THERE A DOCTOR IN THE HOUSE?

One of the traits all great athletes have in common is that they can play in pain. Wrestlers are no exception. Getting into the ring several times a week can certainly be hazardous to your health. The average guy couldn't take the repeated bodyslams and drop kicks, the headlocks and abdominal stretches, not to mention getting hurled over the ropes and out of the ring.

But that's the life of a wrestler and some of them have really shown valor beyond the call of duty. One of the most amazing instances of the show going on despite injury occurred some thirty years ago. A young wrestler named Bob Boyer was trying to make a name for himself. He was willing to wrestle anyone at any time and anywhere.

"No one worked harder than I did," Boyer once said. "I've had bumps, bruises, and broken bones all over my body and I've wrestled from Canada to Mexico. I've wrestled in towns that were so small they weren't even on the map. To get to some of these places I've driven thousands of miles. I've been scorched in the desert and trapped in blizzards. All I ever wanted to do was make it to the big time."

But the road to the big time was paved with obstacles. When Bob Boyer traveled to Mexico in 1956, the things he had to overcome should have earned him a place in the Wrestling Hall of Fame right then and there. He was there for three months. He spoke no Spanish and said it was the loneliest time of his life. He traveled in old buses, in jeeps, and even by mule. The fans looked at him as a villain and sometimes made him fear for his life. But not even that was the real reason Bob Boyer was special.

During the early part of his tour, he injured his left ankle. He was traveling the small towns and there was no doctor available, so he treated the injury as best he could. Night after night he wrestled, while the weakened ankle throbbed with pain. Some nights the pain was almost unbearable, but Bob Boyer kept fulfilling his commitments.

Finally the tour ended and Boyer returned to the States. The ankle was still hurting and extremely swollen. Now Boyer went to a doctor immediately.

"I needed an operation right away," he said. "The ankle had to be reset and the ligaments repaired. To put it simply, I'd been wrestling for three straight months on a fractured ankle and torn ligaments!"

Though the ankle was never quite the same, it healed

enough for Boyer to continue wrestling. The amazing part is how he kept going with the injury. It's hard to visualize an athlete in another sport being able to do the same thing. So for Bob Boyer, it was a truly incredible feat.

THE STRANGE BETRAYAL OF TERRY TAYLOR

Friendships in professional wrestling have always proved very fragile. It's not unusual to suddenly find two grapplers, who had been friends and even partners, facing each other from opposite sides of the ring. And for some reason, when these friendships shatter, the resulting clash is more brutal and violent than is normally the case.

A recent example was the shattered friendship between Steve Williams and Terry Taylor. Williams was an ex-football star, a huge man weighing nearly 300 pounds. A native of Tulsa, Oklahoma, he had played briefly with the New Jersey Generals of the United States Football League, then turned to wrestling.

Williams was always a rough, tough customer. His high school football coach watched his style of play and quickly nicknamed him Doctor Death. The coach meant it as a compliment, but the nickname carried

Terry Taylor seems to be saying "I want you!" to his former friend, Steve Williams, who stole Taylor's championship medal.

over to the ring, and it was a compliment no longer, except maybe in the mind of Steve Williams.

Early in his career, Williams befriended another young wrestler, the popular Terry Taylor. Though their styles were different, the two became friends, taught each other, and often wrestled together as a team. Then Terry Taylor got a break, a chance to wrestle for the Mid-South Television championship. The champion at the time was Krusher Krushchev, and nobody liked him except maybe his mother. Williams was in Taylor's corner the night of the match, ready to lend his friend any support he might need.

The match was brutal and vicious and ended in a victory for neither man. Since Krushchev didn't lose, officials were set to give the championship medal back to him. But when they went to retrieve it, they found that Steve Williams was clutching it in his huge hands.

"Let Terry and Krusher meet again," he roared. "There was no winner tonight. So I'll hold this medal and give it to the winner of their next match, even if it's that rat Krushchev. But no one earned it tonight, so I'll keep it safe and sound."

At the time, no one thought much about it, especially when Williams said there weren't enough men to take it away from him. Why not let him keep it? After all, he would undoubtedly keep his word and give it to the winner of the rematch. So Steve Williams took the championship medal home with him.

The rematch between Taylor and Krushchev was another brutal battle, only this time the popular Taylor emerged a clear winner. After celebrating in the ring, Taylor looked to his friend for the medal.

"I don't have it," Steve Williams said. "I left it home, but I'll give it to you as soon as I can."

Taylor nodded, a little puzzled, but still trusting his friend. Yet when several more weeks passed and he still didn't get the medal he had earned with his blood and sweat, Terry Taylor began to wonder. Finally he demanded the medal and so did Mid-South officials. That's when they realized for the first time that Steve Williams had something else in mind.

"Anyone who wants this medal will have to defeat me for it," Williams exclaimed. "And that includes Terry Taylor. I'm not giving it up."

The news came as a shock to everyone. It was one of the few times in wrestling history that a championship emblem had been claimed by possession, not won or lost in the ring. And for whatever his reasons, the act of stealing Terry Taylor's medal completely changed Steve Williams, in both his outlook on his sport and his perception by the fans.

"I'm the real champion," he proclaimed. "This is the beginning of a whole new era in wrestling. Now Doctor Death's reign of terror is beginning and everyone, including Terry Taylor, is going to find out just why I have that name."

What makes a good man turn bad and what causes close friendships to splinter? It's hard to say, but it is not all that uncommon in the incredible world of professional wrestling.

JUST AN ODD JOB
HERE AND THERE

One of the most popular series of movies in recent years are the James Bond films. Moviegoers everywhere are familiar with British Agent 007, whether he is played by Sean Connery or Roger Moore. One of the earliest and most popular of the Bond films was *Goldfinger,* and it can still be seen both on television and in theaters.

But how many people realize that one of the major roles in *Goldfinger* was played by one of the roughest, toughest, most feared wrestlers in the world? His real name was Harold Sakata, but wrestling fans everywhere knew him as Tosh Togo, a native of Japan who was a master of mayhem in the ring.

In *Goldfinger,* Togo played a deaf-mute character named Odd Job, the right-hand man to the film's villain, Auric Goldfinger. Odd Job dispatched death and destruction the way Tosh Togo dispatched opponents in the ring. Among other things, Odd Job wore a kind of derby hat with a razor-sharp metal brim. He threw it like a frisbee and with deadly accuracy.

During a climactic scene, James Bond and Odd Job staged one of the great fight scenes in movie history. As was sometimes the case in the ring, Tosh Togo dealt out most of the punishment, but was finally defeated. In the film, Odd Job administered a savage beating to Bond at Fort Knox, where much of the gold reserves of the United States were kept. Goldfinger was trying to steal the gold.

Odd Job's derby hat had lodged between some metal bars, and when he went to retrieve it in order to finish Bond off, agent 007 managed to touch a live wire to the bars, electrocuting Odd Job. Making the film was a fun experience for Tosh Togo, who said the poise he acquired through wrestling enabled him to make a smooth transition to the world of motion pictures.

"I can thank wrestling for eliminating any fear I might have had," he said. "Because I've wrestled before large crowds all over the world, I wasn't the least stagestruck. I had a great deal of confidence right from the beginning."

It was also wrestling that helped Tosh Togo get the role. The daughter of one of the studio heads saw Togo wrestling and right away thought he would make a great Odd Job. She told her father who arranged for an interview, then an audition. The rest, as they say, is history.

Despite the film's huge success, Tosh Togo found

himself longing to return to the
pounder realized that wrestling was a way or
wasn't quite ready to abandon.

"Tell the people back in the United States that I'll be
as big and as bad as ever when I return," he said. "And
I can't wait!"

For Tosh Togo, the lure of the ring was still great.
That's the incredible part. Despite starring in a major
motion picture, he longed to return to wrestling. His
movie role was just . . . well . . . another odd job.

SHALL WE DANCE?

In the macho world of wrestling, most grapplers take a he-man approach to their sport. Ask any wrestler what is going to happen when he faces a certain opponent, and he'll likely tell you in no uncertain terms how he is going to destroy his adversary. No question about it.

Yet there was once a wrestler whose approach was entirely different. He entered the ring with ballet slippers on his feet and wearing pink or baby blue trunks. At the beginning of a match he would literally dance around the ring, doing classical ballet steps, jumping and turning, and generally interpreting whatever mood he was in through dance.

His name was Ricki Starr and his opponents learned quickly that it wasn't wise to make fun of his attire or his dance routine. For Starr could handle himself very well in the ring, and his dance training made him one of the most acrobatic of grapplers, with unique holds and

maneuvers such as "The Big Dipper," "The Star
Roll," and "Shooting Star."

Starr also had a different background from most
grapplers. He attended Purdue University as a drama
major and had the lead role in several stage produc-
tions. Yet he already had a love of wrestling and was an
amateur champion at the same time that he was a
budding actor and dancer. Before becoming a professional wrestler in 1952, Ricki Starr had already danced
with several ballet companies, and he decided to bring
his love of dance into the ring with him.

"The first time I did it was in Amarillo, Texas," Starr
said, "and I was really nervous about it. The crowd was
mainly oil workers and cowboys, and a few of them
began riding me at the beginning. But most liked it.
Before the night was over they were all applauding."

Of course, Ricki Starr also used his dancing to rile
his opponents. He would often go into a series of
complicated dance maneuvers, and while his opponents watched and wondered, Ricki would suddenly
dance across the ring and give the other man a playful
slap in the face. The fans loved it, and Ricki's opponents would be angered to distraction.

But the world of dance and the world of wrestling
were not always compatible, especially in the mind of
Ricki Starr. To solve this dilemma, he became one of
the first professional athletes to visit a psychiatrist
with his problems, then talk freely about it.

"I think I'm the first professional athlete to work out
his emotional problems in a scientific manner. There

were things about dance bothering me, but they were hidden deep inside. It had something to do with the prejudices against ballet that I encountered years earlier. What the psychiatrist did was instill and reinforce the idea that dancing and wrestling are separate, but harmonious."

So Ricki Starr continued to do his own unique thing in the ring. He was a top attraction in the late 1950s and 1960s, an outstanding wrestler who proved that wrestlers don't have to be tough guys . . . at least not all the time.

THE INCREDIBLE EIGHTH WONDER OF THE WORLD

In the 1930s, a wrestler came on the scene who defied belief. They called him Man Mountain Dean and he weighed about 400 pounds. He was the first of the so-called giant wrestlers and a foreshadowing of what was to come. But even Man Mountain Dean would look small next to a man who wrestles today, an incredible athlete billed as the Eighth Wonder of the World.

He is a French Canadian called Andre the Giant, and he stands 7'4" tall and weighs nearly 500 pounds. What's even more amazing is that Andre is a gentle man who appreciates some of the more delicate things in life, such as gourmet cooking. He has even appeared on nationwide talk shows where he has discussed cooking instead of wrestling and has prepared some of his favorite dishes in front of the camera.

In the squared circle, however, the Giant is not so delicate. Wrestling all over the world, Andre has never

It's easy to see why no man has ever defeated Andre the Giant by a pin or submission. The huge Canadian stands 7′4″ tall and weighs nearly 500 pounds. Here he dwarfs his good friend and fellow grappler, the muscular Tony Atlas.

been pinned and never forced to submit. The only times he hasn't emerged a winner have been caused by disqualifications. Because of his great size and immense popularity, Andre has always been a target of rulebreakers, and this has made it difficult for him.

"When I started wrestling I always depended on my size and strength," Andre has said. "But as I became more experienced I learned more and more about scientific wrestling. Unfortunately, many of my opponents use brute force and all kinds of rulebreaking tactics against me. Because of this, I will often fight back the same way, and that makes every match a bitter struggle."

In recent years, more and more wrestlers have come after Andre the Giant. There isn't a man in the pro ranks who wouldn't want to be the first to pin this living legend. As a consequence, Andre has been in much more difficult matches against bigger and stronger foes. Some fans think he is taking too much punishment. But the brutal matches have led to feuds which the fans seem to love. And Andre certainly won't run from a fight.

"I've never started a feud and I don't like them," Andre has said. "But there are certain people gunning for me and I'm not hard to find."

The most vicious of these feuds began in early 1985. Though he wasn't legally defeated in a match, the Giant found himself "ambushed" by Big John Studd, Ken Patera, and their insidious manager, Bobby "The Brain" Heenan. What they did to Andre was perhaps the most humiliating thing anyone could have done to such a proud man. They cut his long dark hair!

It takes an awful lot to really make Andre angry. But this cowardly act was going too far. The Giant vowed revenge, and said it wouldn't be pretty. Defeating Studd and Patera as part of a three-man tag team wasn't nearly good enough. Andre wanted more. Heenan hadn't been there that night, so when the Giant finally met Patera one on one, and saw the Brain in Patera's corner, he sensed his time had come.

Patera, a former Olympic weightlifter, fancies himself the world's strongest man. But in the hands of Andre the Giant, he had the strength of a puppet. Andre began tossing him around the ring. When Heenan began taunting the Giant, Andre turned his attention to the rulebreaking manager.

That gave Patera a chance to recover and he attacked Andre from behind. The match was quickly turning ugly, especially when Heenan began slamming the Giant with his walking stick. For a minute it looked as if the big guy was in trouble. But somehow he managed to get a hand on Heenan and dragged the manager into the ring. What happened next was one of the most bizarre sights ever seen in a ring.

Andre the Giant hoisted Bobby Heenan above his head and began using the manager as a human club. He pounded Ken Patera with his own manager! Andre seemed possessed with superhuman strength as he used Heenan to batter Patera to the canvas. Then he tossed the dazed manager on top of the dazed wrestler and pinned them both as the huge crowd went wild. Still, Andre wanted more.

"I am going to continue to punish these men whenever and wherever I find them," he said. "My revenge will only be complete when all three of them retire from professional wrestling."

There was still the matter of Big John Studd. No slouch in the size department himself, Big John stands 6'10" and weighs close to 400 pounds. But he's still no Giant, and Andre vowed he would bodyslam Studd or retire from wrestling. The two met on March 31, 1985, as part of the huge Wrestlemania extravaganza at Madison Square Garden in New York before some twenty-two thousand five hundred fans.

Studd was making his usual claims that no one had ever bodyslammed him and offered the Giant $15,000 if he could do it. The match began with Studd managing to drop Andre to the canvas and getting on top. But the Giant's thirst for revenge was still strong, his rage growing, and he threw Studd off as if he were a paper doll.

With the fans screaming and roaring, Andre wasted no time. He bear-hugged Studd, pinning his arms to his side, squeezing harder and harder to weaken his opponent. Then he casually lifted Studd over his head, paused to smile at the TV cameras, then bodyslammed his enemy to the canvas with a vengeance!

Studd was finished. The fans roared as Andre grabbed the dufflebag that contained the $15,000 bounty. The Giant began tossing some of the cash to the ringside patrons when the defeated Studd sneaked up, grabbed the bag, and ran out of the ring. But Andre only laughed harder. The money didn't mean anything to him. He had beaten Big John Studd, bodyslammed him, and he continued to mete out the revenge he had promised.

To many fans, Andre the Giant stands head and shoulders over all other wrestlers. He is loved the world over and has proved once again that he is one of the most incredible and amazing figures in all of sport.

GEE, THANKS, DAD!

To paraphrase an old saying, you can take the wrestler out of the ring, but you can't take the heart out of the wrestler, especially when the honor of his son is at stake. Recently two legendary champions returned to the ring to help out sons who were following in their footsteps. One of the retired champs did it on an official basis, the other on an impromptu one. But in both cases the fans loved seeing their favorites back again.

The legendary Verne Gagne had been a champion for many years, holding the AWA belt on and off for some two decades. The Minnesota native tapered off his activities in the 1970s and retired for good in the early 1980s. At least he thought it was for good. For in 1985 Verne Gagne found a good reason for a return. In fact, it was the best reason a man could have.

He decided to help his son, Greg, who had followed his father's footsteps to become a fine wrestler in his own right. But in 1985 Greg became embroiled in a feud with the nasty Nick Bockwinkel and the evil Mr. Saito, and those two had launched several brutal sneak attacks on young Gagne.

Finally Verne had seen enough. He challenged Bockwinkel and Saito to a tag-team match, claiming he would come out of retirement to join his son. The villains agreed, figuring the aging Gagne would be dead meat. More than 16,000 fans packed the St. Paul Civic Center to witness the match, and it turned out to be a real slam-bang affair.

Many of the fans who loved Verne Gagne were concerned about their hero. They didn't want to see him hurt.

"It's not like I just had three weeks of training," Verne said. "I have 30 years of experience behind me."

The Gagnes showed they meant business by storming the ring and attacking Bockwinkel and Saito as the fans roared. Veteran Verne, it seems, had learned some new rules. Once the match officially began, Greg was in control until he made the mistake of turning his back. That's when Bockwinkel and Saito double-teamed him and had him in deep trouble until he managed to tag his father. Verne came on like a hurricane looking for a place to land. He threw chops, drop-kicks, and bodyslams, and finally got Bockwinkel in his famous sleeper. He would have had the match right there if Saito hadn't clobbered him from behind.

But as Bockwinkel lifted the stunned Verne into a backbreaker, Greg paid them back by sneaking in for a drop-kick, sending Bockwinkel to the canvas with Verne on top of him. The veteran recovered his composure quickly and applied the pin, ending the match. The fans went wild. They had witnessed the return of a living legend and hometown hero, a concerned father who returned to the ring to help his son. It was an amazing and heartwarming night.

The other return was an unexpected one. It occurred during the Wrestlemania spectacular at Madison Square Garden in March of 1985. One of the preliminary bouts featured David Sammartino, son of the legendary champion Bruno Sammartino. David was wrestling Brutus Beefcake, who was accompanied by his manager, "Luscious" Johnny Valiant.

Though Beefcake attempted to take charge early, young David turned the tables, using the great strength inherited from his father. But then Beefcake got lucky. He managed to get David out of the ring and there he got help from Valiant, who bodyslammed young Sammartino on the hard cement.

But Valiant didn't count on one thing. Bruno Sammartino was at ringside and he wasn't about to watch this happen. As the crowd roared itself into a frenzy, the great champion charged at Valiant and began slugging it out with him. Valiant tried to escape into the ring, but Bruno chased after him and began punching and kicking him. The referee tried to restore order, but Valiant and Beefcake wanted no part of this great, great wrestler. Instead of resuming the match, they beat a hasty retreat and the bout was declared a draw.

But it was worth it to the fans, the chance to see a living legend back in action. It was also good to see that some old-fashioned values are still with us. Both Verne Gagne and Bruno Sammartino risked their own safety and possible injury to come to the aid of their sons. It's the kind of thing that could only happen in the unpredictable sport of professional wrestling.

WHAT'S IN A NAME?

Perhaps more than any other sport, wrestling has the strangest names, nicknames, and identities. How some of these wrestlers got their names is a story in itself. One of the oddest was a wrestler known as the Zebra Kid.

His real name was George Bollas, and that was no secret. Yet he wrestled with a mask, a mask that had the stripes of a zebra embroidered into it. Wrestling all over the world from 1947 to 1968, the Zebra Kid was one of the best known of the topflight grapplers. He didn't wear the mask when he first turned pro, after an incredibly successful amateur career which saw him win the National Intercollegiate, National AAU, and Big Ten heavyweight titles. As a collegian at Ohio State, he never lost a fall.

But shortly after he turned pro he came to New York to make a name for himself. Then in a match with Mattie Mario, a brawl broke out, followed by a riot.

Bollas was subsequently barred from wrestling in the New York Area. To conceal his identity at that time, he donned a mask and headed south, wrestling as the Intercollegiate Dark Secret. But that just didn't seem to fit. It was when he finally wound up in Hollywood that the Zebra Kid emerged. But people would never guess how he got the name.

It was because George Bollas was a big man, nearly a 300-pounder, and he had gained the weight very quickly when he was at Ohio State.

"From gaining all that weight so fast I had stretch marks all over my body. The marks looked like stripes and even in those days the guys would call me 'Zeeb'! So it seemed like a natural thing to call myself the Zebra Kid."

That's how the Zebra Kid was born. And by the time he was forced out of wrestling by an eye injury, fans the world over knew and feared this powerful man with the zebra-striped mask. But how many ever knew that he got his name because he gained a lot of weight in a short amount of time? It was a strange way to find a nickname and a professional identity.

WRESTLING ROCKS INTO THE EIGHTIES

The 1980s have presented professional wrestling in a whole new light. The sport has come full circle and has even returned to prime-time television, a spot it once held back in the 1950s. Wrestling stars have become media personalities, though not without controversy, and a strange alliance has been forged between the world of the squared circle and rock and roll music.

Leading the way to this alliance is Cyndi Lauper, who became a music superstar with her big hits "Girls Just Wanna Have Fun," "All Through the Night," and "Time After Time." Besides attending many matches and managing women's champ Wendi Richter, Cyndi Lauper has given her wrestling friends and enemies major roles in her rock videos.

In fact, when she produced a video for the song, "The Goonies 'R' Good Enough," she had the following cast of characters included: Captain Lou Albano,

Rowdy Roddy Piper, The Iron Sheik, Freddie Blassie, Nikolai Volkoff, Wendi Richter, and the Fabulous Moolah. Imagine putting all those people into the ring at the same time!

The growing popularity of pro wrestling has also brought much more attention from the news media. Several reporters have been injured by mat stars demonstrating holds such as the sleeper, or by wrestlers angered by accusations that their sport is rigged. These incidents have served to show the power of these men and the seriousness with which they view their chosen profession.

Then there is the Hulk, perhaps the most popular man wrestling today. How many fans know, for instance, that this mountain of a man began wrestling under the name of Sterling Golden? Not too many, because today Hulk Hogan is a media personality all his own. He had a role in *Rocky III,* with Sylvester Stallone, and appeared with who else but Cyndi Lauper as a presenter on the nationally televised Academy Awards broadcast.

There are also videos on the market containing some of the Hulk's toughest matches, and also a new cartoon show depicting the Hulk as America's newest hero. The Hulk's picture has appeared on the cover of many national magazines. All this has served to make wrestling more popular than ever.

The sport has certainly come a long way from the days of crackling paper in front of the microphone to simulate the breaking of bones. Now, simulation isn't necessary. Fans can see for themselves—in person, on television, and on videos. The performers are great athletes, huge men, and the action is fast and furious. Fan reaction is more intense than anywhere else. Pro wrestling has come of age in what may be the most amazing phenomenon of our time.

So stay tuned. It's coming at you. And there's a lot more of it just around the corner. Don't be surprised in upcoming years if there is a man larger than Andre the Giant, more hated than Roddy Piper, and tougher than Hulk Hogan. For the incredible world of professional wrestling never runs out of surprises.

About the Author

BILL GUTMAN has been an avid sports fan ever since he can remember. A free-lance writer for fourteen years, he has done profiles and bios of many of today's sports heroes. Although Mr. Gutman likes all sports, he has written mostly about baseball and football. Currently, he lives in Poughquag, New York, with his wife, two stepchildren, seven dogs, and five birds.